A Life's

Tapestry

A Life's
Tapestry

PATRICIA STANWAY

A LIFE'S TAPESTRY

iUniverse books may be ordered through booksellers or by contacting:

iUniverse
1663 Liberty Drive
Bloomington, IN 47403
www.iuniverse.com
844-349-9409

ISBN: 978-1-6632-1967-1 (sc)
ISBN: 978-1-6632-1969-5 (hc)
ISBN: 978-1-6632-1968-8 (e)

Print information available on the last page.

iUniverse rev. date: 03/29/2021

I dedicate this book to my beautiful daughter Lisa, and grandchildren Scarlett and Ziaray. I love you with all that I am.

Acknowledgement

I wish to thank my dear friend V. for his heartfelt support and encouragement over the years.

To Cristina, thank you for being with me on this journey, and for the hours spent together sifting thru paper, and hours of amazing conversation.

To Doug and Sue for your friendship, and sharing a place of refuge and inspiration.

To all my friends over the years, who encouraged me, I thank you all. I am blessed to have you in my life.

To my brother Philip, I love you! Thank you for always encouraging me.

Sensuality

Discovering Desire

It was truly wonderous, and it could never be forgotten—
an eruption of passion never before had I unleashed.
A knowing that, deep within, I can never go back;
a pulsating need of you that for all times will never cease;
a devastation encountered never before; an intimacy never touched.
A fierce, lustful desire with a thirst that can never be quenched;
a toxic potion flowing, and my body crying out in the night
for the need in us to be always together, fused in light.

I circle above our bed of scattered flowers and smell the potent perfume,
floating higher and higher as your lips touch mine, devouring me.
As your tidal wave erupts through my body in motion, completing
nature's thrust,
you take me where you will, and I totally surrender,
to be ravished in each and every way.
If need turned to stars, I feel your starlight within me,
saturated with a burning nectar of touch,
and as my trust grows, as the crescendo plays to the ballet of white orbs,
I become raw and explode into the prism kaleidoscope.

Hungry for Love

Please take me home and undress me slowly,
at your leisure; please make no haste.
Take me slowly as each part of my flesh is exposed,
nibble, caress with your tongue, devour all of me,
savor my taste, feel the essence of lust emerge from me,
secreting bubbling liquid of white within.

And as your tongue probes deep into my mouth,
feel the tremors of my soul,
and yearning of the embers to ignite, feel it begin.
Feel the honey within as we merge into one
and soar to heights that in our essence and minds
will forever linger.

Love

Fire

A single touch from you, and my body responds;
a flame is ignited, the lava bubbles,
and the anticipation of a glow secretes,
waiting for the nectar to arrive.
At the moment we will both become reunited,
the flames dance and tantalize within my core,
and I feel the searing heat deep inside,
teasing, tugging at the insides of my being,
saturating my whole body with a deep desire,
submerging me into a sea of milk.
Joining together with deep, throaty, lusting cries,
I feel the pull as a lotus flower opening to the heavens above.
I feel the rhythm of your body ride up, and I am above the waves;
you pulse within me, deep inside,
and the want of yours is torn from me,
as the surrender is imminent
and our very essence is burst open.

Reflection

Love has no other desire than to fulfill itself,
but if you should love,
then let this be your only desire.

To melt and be as a running brook
that sings its melody to the night,
to know the pain of too much tenderness,
to be wounded by your own understanding of love,
and to bleed willingly and joyfully.

To wake at dawn with a winged heart
and give thanks for another day of loving,
to rest at the noon hour and meditate love's ecstasy,
to return home in the evening with warm gratitude.

And then to sleep with a prayer
for the beloved in your heart
and a song of praise upon your lips.

Gentle Thoughts of You

I wish to feel the gentleness of your fingers upon my face,
and I crave your mouth on mine,
your lips to tantalize each and every intimate place.
I wish to feel your head close to mine,
your hand laid gently on my breast.

I wish to touch you and tease you sensuously
as my fingers caress your chest.
I wish to feel your long, slender legs
and your hardened thighs at my side.

I want to see your eyes as we make love,
both for us to give with nothing to hide.
I want to love you, as I do,
in each and every special way.
And I wish for the company of you,
with me throughout my life every day.

Thinking of You Tonight

It's a truly wondrous feeling that overcomes you
when you feel that surge of warmth sear through your mind,
and it's lovely when you think of the man you love
in the loneliness of the night, the comfort that you can find.

You inhale the freshness of the shower and the perfume of the soap
mingled with the smell of freshly minted breath,
and as you lay basking in the want of that moment,
you are there within the walls of heaven,
and at that moment you would not even argue with death.

I remember it all—the touch of his skin,
and the silkiness of his stomach and thighs as I explore with my fingers,
and when we are spent with the love and beautiful thoughts we say,
and feel
those echoes of desire dance and linger.

Love is indeed a wondrous thing;
it is the only essence that is truly secreted solely for the heart.
And after a lifetime of searching, the gift has been given.
I am me, and from my love of he and I, we will never be apart.

As a Flower

I am joyfully caressed, when warmed by the sunlight;
my petals glow with the brightness of that moment
and last even through the darkness of the night.
Yet if I should be denied that warmth and be placed alone in the shade,
my petals would dry, and no more would I be immersed in vitality,
for my colors and inspiration would fade.

Love is like a flower for the special few:
their need is to always bask in the light of the sun,
and when no longer is that warmth generated constantly,
the coolness will seep into their hearts,
and it is as if the essence of love had never really begun.

Unsure

I cannot understand why he chooses to be detached.
I always saw love as an emotion that was seemingly always attached.
Maybe it's unwise to connect with an immune mind of emotion;
it's probably better to relish in the starkness of knowledge
and external caring, finding another resting place for my devotion.
But I do not wish for sterility, only to collide in a moment of passion.
I need the nearness and acceptance of a union of two souls
in spirit, mentally and with a given compassion.

Be Kind

For some souls, Christmas is of no more.
For them each day is misery, and for them there are no gifts in store.
As we laugh with joy, with our loved ones around the Christmas tree,
we must send our hearts, prayers, and thoughts for the ones not so fortunate
as you and me.
The aged, with all their memories of Christmases gone past,
reminisce in their minds, hanging on to the only thread of warmth and laughter,
each one in his or her own way amid the despair and loneliness,
fantasies that will be needed again, for now and ever after.
Reach out to these lonely souls with eyes of light and love,
and leave the imprint of God's divinity.

Family

Grandad Ben Franklin

As I slowly walked among the grass
and reveled on the mildness of the night,
I felt my eyes drawn by some unearthly force to the stars,
which to my vision glowed unnaturally bright.
In an instance, I was breathless as a wetness touched my face,
surprising my mind that it had begun to rain.
But then I tasted the salt in my mouth and accepted the tears of sadness
burning down my face, for I knew I would never in this life see you
again.
For so very long, I've wanted to talk to you and see the wisdom in your
eyes;
I've needed to hear that one reliable truth,
which always remained untouched by devilish lies.
I've loved you then, now and always,
missing your presence every second that you've been gone.
Yet deep inside my soul, I'm content with the knowledge
you are at peace, and I will finally accept that it was right,
and God's will had to be done.
For every child, there is a gift, to share a walk with their grandfather
side by side.
A touch of an aged hand and the surge of warmth that comes from him
within,
the beauty of a togetherness for which even time will never surpass,
for it will be encased in the walls of your heart.
And each and every memory never fades,
just knowingly lies silent for a while but never dies,
even when you are apart.

Music

Water Music

The raptures of Handel float through the air hauntingly
yet bring warmth to the chill of the night.
And as I lie back, I am lulled by the sensuous caress of the water
arousing my skin to sheer delight.

A wave of peacefulness and serenity invades my senses,
and a wonderous glow rampages through my mind,
secreting visions of true wonders and mystic charm traveling side by
side.

And as if afraid that I may not envision all that is there,
I open eagerly, my eyes wide.
The gentle strings of a violin caress my chords of emotions;
the melodies oozing through my body,
lingering invitingly, a soft soothing lotion.

Each note selected with a special delicacy,
bringing unto my soul an absorption of serenity with intense pleasure,
a concerto of love created for all the world to hear.
Music is so much inner discovery, it brings awareness,
it soothes the nerves, delights the mind, and is intoxicating.
It's peaceful as well as unleashing at the same moment,
gentle turbulence of life's eternal tears.

Searching

A Message from Within

An openness exists between us that is a miracle of love in itself,
for that I am happy within. Alas, even with that, it seems that there are always
words from my lips that just don't know how to begin.
It's more than a need, it's more than a want or a yearning desire.
It's what life's essence is within my soul.
It's a simple formula that ignites my own eternal fires.
I have found in you what my life means,
a permanency from which I would never need to stray.
My love for you is as impenetrable as infinity is to man,
and as awesome and as beautiful as the cosmos,
with its moon and stars and kaleidoscopes of light.
You will, if you so desire, now and always absorb a force
that will forever cherish and protect me,
with a flame that will burn forever bright.
The powerful existence of you is deep within me and
I am content with that knowledge.
That with us there is that divine power directing me,
presenting me with a gift for only my soul to see.
It is in the interest of man, and life itself, that God in all his wisdom
has granted to me the gift of immortality, simply by showing you to me.
Come stay with me, my friend, and let us live together
in complete harmony and love.
A privilege of essence sent from above and each and every day.
Let us glory in that wonderful thought that we have been caressed by one of
God's messengers, a serene friend of love and purity,
the white bird of peace, the dove.

Finding My Father

Where has the glow gone? Did it flee into yesterday?
How did it move unseen, or was it quickly whisked away?
As a child born of the earth, I was never sure where I belonged,
but will I find my father? Maybe I was wrong.

Through the darkness, I feel the warmth and rise to meet the sun.
He reached out with his hands to me, and now my walk has begun.
I know that I am one with one, even when on earth I stand alone.
I need to kiss the life of my extension to set me on my journey,
as a union until I die.

Loss and Pain

Remembrance of
Someone You Love

As I sat in my rocking chair built by your loving hands,
I clutched the lace handkerchief to my face,
and through the tears in my over bright eyes, I envisioned that heartfelt
place.
The small babbling brook at the end of the lane,
where you and I had stolen many a kiss.
And the old elm tree, where we had carved our love in its bark,
stood tall and strong no more.
There were so many changes, so much one did miss.

The old garden gate, which always squeaked—
remember the one you had always meant to fix one day?
And the weeds growing in between the flagstones,
nature's incessant chaos of beauty on display.
The cottage still stood where we had laughed and loved
for so many wonderful years, and now the cemetery where you lie,
peaceful among your petals of love, and where I had shed so many tears.
Well, my love, these memories have given me so much warmth and joy,
as without you I had to live out my life.
But now God has visited me, and my journey had to begin,
and I rejoiced in the knowledge that once more
we would become man and wife.

Hidden Ache

Seventeen years ago seems to most a very long time;
many wouldn't be able to even recall.
But for the woman walking along the beach,
it will remain forever locked deep within her soul.
I am sure that there are many women in this world
who know the pain, yet to try and talk about it,
they don't know where to begin.

I can talk about it and will never truly want to reexperience
the feelings of that terrible day, the Tuesday morning at eleven forty-five,
that a nurse took a small bundle of warmth
from my arms and whisked him away.
I remember the days of labor, convincing myself
that God was punishing me for the terrible things I had done.
My mother sitting beside me, thinking that I was about to die,
telling me that I deserved to be punished.
At that particular moment, I wish she had been right; I do not lie.

I truly must have lived in a vacuum of numbness and confusion,
because I died a little inside each day as it passed.
I remember the looks and the talk.
I remember the navy-and-red coat that never fastened at the front,
how I held my head as I had to walk the gauntlet of wagging tongues
of shame.

My Shaping

I realized how cruel a family can be at an early age,
a nonexistence of compassion or caring.
Even as a child, I felt unloved, not understood;
I recoiled and lived in a small world of fantasy and pain.
And as the child was taken away from me without my permission,
for me life has continued to take.

Maybe until this moment, I closed myself
to all the emotions out there in the world,
but now I am ready to take that first step in risking, living.
I can revel in the joy of loving without as everything,
and everyone I ever loved had been taken away.
I fear that this will happen because finally I am devoid of feeling
I am alive, but not living. How can I possibly love if I detest myself?
Can I finally be brave enough and boldly live openly every day?

My Lost Son

Seventeen years appear, for some, a very long time;
for some, the occurrences appear dim.
But for me, the passage of time has appeared short,
and when memories stir, the feelings are grim.
The guilt will remain within me until the day God decides to bring me home,
but until that day comes to pass, the feelings and tearful memories of sorrow persist.
There are, I know, many who carry this burden, hidden deep within,
needing to talk with their husband or friend, not knowing how or where to begin.
To talk of a loss that was not under your control, a child carried within your womb of life,
to describe the birth of a child as a terrible day, can only be understood if, within a few days, that warm bundle that you held, you fed, is ripped from your arms and whisked away.
A brutal mistake made in ignorance and confusion.
Feeling so unwanted as a child, you mistook lust for love,
your desperate need for arms of warmth to enfold you,
just as the softness of the petals of a rose and the winged feathers of a dove.
A child having a child, and knowing your unworthiness,
believing you are the spawn of the devil, cruelty of words echoing from the family you belong to, no compassion.
They knew nothing and cared less of the hurt hidden deep within the child of sixteen,
and they knew nothing of the strength that it would take, for me to endure the darkest tongues.
To hold your head up as you walked. knowing that behind those false smiles,
there was disgust and malicious name-calling as they talked with judgment.

Disconnection

One more broken promise,
one more bubble vaporized by tears,
slowly eroding the essence that swirls within.
Many lonely nights, no solid intent,
just acted out of desperation to fight the enveloping fear.

Values changing in the moments of time,
separating one from another;
hands reaching out for love and warmth,
a union needed from the being of man.

No interconnectedness desired from your partner,
no longer a friend, no longer a lover.
Confusion in the presence of now,
a longing for the values and feelings frozen from when it began.

Deception

A gentle kiss, the scent of his skin intoxicates my senses,
and I grow weak and close my eyes.
The soft hands along my thighs cause turbulence within the core of
my mind,
and I want him, refusing to see the truth in his lies.

To love in vain is to breathe unclean air
and be tortured from deep within.
It's the decay of beauty,
it's when the slow death of life is about to begin.

Do not allow this to pass unheeded in your brain and heart.
Sever the connection before it becomes deceased.
Create the strengths to tear it apart.

Discovery

Transformation

An exodus of heat evaporates around my body
as the memory stirs within.
The heady sensations of delight
ooze through the seeds of my mind, settling deep within,
clinging tightly to every fiber of my being.
It awaits with anticipation, as the transformation is about to begin.
My skin feels the touch of life,
its essence felt for the very first time,
and my being is scattered into a world of stars and ethereal light.
Caught within a whirl of sensuous exotic potions,
I swallow willingly and drown, submitting
my essence to explode beyond the cosmic frontier
as the calm of the day is transformed
into the mystic, erotic wonders of the night.

Lost

If my needs are not the same
and cannot be understood, how or why by another,
then let me search the land for the light,
warmth, and constant nurturing of a would-be lover.

Wanting to grow yet not knowing why,
wanting to live forever yet not knowing why you have to die.
Needing to love, understanding why, and knowing who,
yet the road is hard and long.

Needing to be vulnerable and let go,
yet terrified that you might be wrong.
So many journeys we embark on in our short lives, on this planet earth,
yet never seeming quite to getting it all together,
never cherishing our own worth.

Feelings, emotions, hurt, pain, so much chaos
do we inflict upon our awesome minds.
All of us in desperate search for the peace that can be found in all of us,
yet something we never seem to find.

Essence of Prayer

As I gazed unknowingly to him,
I heard his silent prayer for me,
sent to God one by one from his holy beads.
And suddenly the perfume of flowers drifted into the room,
invading my senses with exhilarating speed,
and the seconds of life are falling down my face in a single tear.
Yet only the sadness of knowing that I will never see you again in this
life
holds a coldness in my heart, but for death itself I hold no fear.
A lightness invades my body, and I feel the elevation to the Lord begin.
Retaining every touch of life, each wondrous experience,
I feel the pulses of memory sink deep within,
but I want to tell them they need not weep,
for even as I step into the beam of light, strong, gentle hands
are guiding me as I walk toward the cosmic gate whisked away.

An Encounter

The night air was frigid as we hurried along the sidewalk,
anxious to shelter from the bitterness of the night.
It was then, through the remnants of our breath, we stopped in awe at
the sight thus to behold:
losing memory of our hands and feet filled with numbness, and the
redness of our faces.
We pressed on with the excitement of children, as magnets drawn to
an aura that appeared to
surround that familiar place.
Their faces were smooth, and eyes gentle as a fawn and as trusting as
a gazelle.
Their long slender arms reached out, and their touch was wonderous,
and we walked forward with the knowledge that humanity and the
planet would fare well.

A Journey

As I gaze through the blackness of my eyes, I am touched by the beauty
of visions I see.
Water bearers walking side by side, scorched by noonday's sun on their
way to the sea.
Sand flies in their faces, gravel protrudes sharply into their bare feet,
but oblivious
they march on.
Hot and dusty, they patiently await their turn to take their fill, and after
one hour,
they return to the valley, and then as if engulfed in the heat of the desert,
they are gone.

I am running, the sand swirling, biting into my face, cruelly stinging
my eyes.
Chiffon floats around my body, its fold wrapping tighter by every move
I make.
Sweat trickles down my spine, between my breasts.
My legs are stiff, my back feels as if it is about to break.
Yet I press on, a compulsion, an instinct giving me direction,
yet not knowing where I go, I crawl relentless in my pursuit,
and the man standing before me is neither my friend nor my foe.
He is a mirage, created by only my eyes.
I fall and sink to the bed of sand.
I see circles of birds, and I know I am about to die.

Fantasy

Invasion of Lust

Flowers and perfumes of nectar, sweetness, invade my open mouth,
essences of cream and silk filling my body with an urge deeply embedded
inside my soul.
Pulsating inside my womb lingers a throbbing knight.
An armor of soft steel, completing his mission as he creates me whole.

Tempting me, drawing me close as I cry out with ecstasy and fright.
A dawning knowledge of being and feeling completed and right.
So beautiful to drown in an intoxicating and enchanting adventure.
A mind drowning in the milk of lust.
Nostrils flare when invaded with that familiar scent.

Nerves sing, chanting in rhyme,
and your body moves, intensifying the heat until it is spent.
I open seductively, welcoming the magnetic pull
as it increases its pitch to glorious devastation, seared with heat.
I drag you deeper within me, searching, probing,
until finally our souls and all its divine fluids secrete.

It's such a frightening discovery,
to consume such an explosive passion and intense want.
To be totally sated, still moist with remembrance, craving a touch.
God help me, for I cannot cease to devour you in my mind
and willingly drown in your touch.

Truth

Elusive Truth

Can I really expect the truth from every person I meet?
Can I really expect a smile from everyone who passes me on the street?
We lie to ourselves, to a father, a sister, a daughter, a brother.
We lie to protect ourselves from pain; we lie to our mother.
The world sometimes seems devoid of love.
We reach out constantly with our hands,
waiting for the warmth of truths insulated glove.
I have tried to find it, but the mouths of men speak with forked tongues.
Eyes are lowered and the pretense rises, uncomfortable with their own
songs.
No truth can they ever tell themselves.
They only see the mirror that reflects from afar, their lies and vanity
arising in
the dark.

Desire

Unbridled Passion

My skin still burns with the touch of you,
and the vibrations of fulfilled desire
only you, my love, have unleashed,
the uncontrollable embers of scorching fires.

I feel your head between my breasts,
your lips moist, teasing their aching buds to readiness.
Tendrils dance a ballet of ecstasy and delight,
consuming me in a vortex of brightness.

My passion is touched by you, and warmth sears through my brain,
exceeding the speed of light.
An explosion of a million fragments of stars in the sky
through eyes glazed by passion.

I see you silhouetted in the night.
My eyes are searching for yours,
and finally, as I come home at that moment,
for you I know I would gladly die.

Airborne

I feel the perspiration clinging to my skin
and feel the arousal of past desires scatter within.
I am hot, and the wetness on my brow travels down my face.
Air in my lungs is expelled as I am transported back in time to that unforgotten place.
The sounds that I hear are the murmurs of my own deep sighs,
and as the fantasies emerge deep within my mind,
I feel the heat sear through my open thighs;
it is getting hotter, and my pulse is in a rapid and free flight.
And I am airborne, drowning in the sensuousness fantasies seen only through my eyes.
I look closer and see the erotic pleasure,
and feel my body move in sensuous delight.
I am traveling faster than the speed of light, and launched,
I explode into a myriad of light deeply outlined in the shadows of the sky.

Introspection

A Message Sent

I stood high on the mountaintop surveying the vastness of a kingdom
from above.
Through my eyes the visions of undulating hills of green, ripples of
water
sparkling in the sunlight, blessing a creation with my love.
The joyous laughter of children touching my heart with pleasing words
of wonder and delight.
Vowing no matter what another human atrocity would be chosen,
I would never allow complete destruction, but against evil all humanity
will struggle.
Yes, some will choose to wear their armor; standing resolute in faith,
they will fight.
The scent of salt that I had scattered across the earth invades my nostrils,
oozing through my being and intoxicating my brain,
and the scent of flowers created with my angels of nature and love
floated through the breeze, a rhapsody of sweet refrain.
The babbling brook slowed as if for a second
to talk to me as it begins its long journey to the sea,
where, with its purpose entwined with another would flow,
rejoicing as it discovered another soul.
And the creatures of the sky would burst into song,
swoop down, and kiss my hand, and of each I knew their name.
And the bees, busily buzzing by,
would sing as they happily gathered their nectar
as they played their magical game.

The Joining

I am drowning in that wondrous emotion called love,
soaring to heights even I could not imagine existed at all.
And this morning, as I sit here, being caressed by Vivaldi,
bringing to my senses concertos of happiness and pleasure,
I see before my eyes the vision of your face
so clearly outlined within the pattern of the kitchen wall,
yet only for a moment am I sitting, quietly alone.
For even as I think of you, I am aware of the nearness
ascending, I'm enveloped into a mist of heady and warm sensation,
clinging to every moment of your caring and tenderness.
It is real and it is good, the way that I feel about you.
It is a dream of a lifetime journey, which some unfortunately never make.
But for me, this miracle is of now, and I am full of joy and happiness,
and as God and all the planets above all gave me that gift,
I have accepted that it is mine to take.
Even as I end one journey, another one begins.
I love you, and I pray the next adventure is for us to take together,
and then another life begins.

Wholeness

A force not like any other thing
has risen and invaded my soul.
A power of such devasting truth,
one that brings you closer to yourself.
A strength not yet matched by another being,
and an awareness that you are finally whole.
It is called life, the meaning of life,
and the reaching out for another to share.
A chance to give a special part to another,
and a chance to let another soul know you care.
A galaxy of stars reflecting lights of hope,
and everlasting unions of love caress the sky with wonderous glow,
as pure as the whiteness and gentleness of a dove.

Reborn

I have passed a boundary of want and attained a completeness
that I felt could not possibly be.
Something touched me deeper than the depths I possess,
and I know ultimately I will emerge for you to clearly see.

I love you with the true embodiment of my being
and have begun the evolution of death.
You have taken me into a world unfamiliar to me,
yet in that place, I will draw my last breath.

A Walk to Heaven and Beyond

As the leaves crunched beneath my feet,
I experienced an inner joy spreading throughout my being,
igniting within me a flame, warming my soul, uplifting me up toward the sky.
The crispness of the night fills my body
with the exhilaration of being so aware of the life within me,
and I felt the power that moved urging me, lifting me above all on high.
I gazed down on the earth, where I had experienced life itself,
and I smiled in remembrance and wished my last farewell to the remnants of
all humankind.
The stars caressed me as they passed my side, floating in an abundance of light and essence.
And I felt the gentleness of the universe reach out and touch me,
pulling me close to the discovery of the wonders it intended me to find.
Then I awoke to see that the dawn had broken through with ethereal glory,
and the birds acknowledged its return with eager glee.
The realization of where I had been and how I had been touched by the souls of
all life would forever rejoice in absorbing the true oneness of me.
Until tomorrow, my love, when you and I will caress all divinity with our love
and know the meaning of our true light.
Until tomorrow, my love, when even in darkness, our beam of life will reach all
corners of the universe and provide that guiding light.

Nature

Godly Homes

Hearts within houses and houses with a heart
that pulsates with the strength of life itself.
A land with riches hidden beneath the soil,
for nature provides an abundance of wealth.

Sturdy, strong houses dotted over the land
with the welcoming of the smoke for any pioneers to see.

A place of peace for those who wish to sweat and strive.
For men who know the laws of nature will oblige,
for they also know what God's will should be.

Invasion of Thoughts

I sit alone in the candlelight,
watching the flames burning warm and bright.
And as the music is playing,
my senses unfold, and I am compelled to write.

I feel elevated and travel within myself,
a knowing of a journey that will be filled with so much love.
My only companion on this pilgrimage
will be peace and wings of a solitary white dove.

My fingers reach out, and the softness of a rose is felt within.
I look into a web held within the trees
and observe the life of a butterfly begin.
I feel a tear fall from the sky,
and I am bathed in the dew of a summer rain.

High in the heavens, the message of migration
and the pulses of life are repeated again and again.
Over a multitude of lands I travel, reveling in the white and brown faces
playing with happiness, nurturing one another in love.
So much wondrous beauty of life do I see,
yet in awe I think that the abundance of nature's hidden secrets of
delight is
endless.

The Realms

A ghost of winter past emerged with fleeting smiles
and a gesture of his hand,
beckoning us forward, and with much trepidation we reach out
and begin that journey to a far-off land.

Dragons and creatures, tall and small,
live on earth alongside us all.
A world of hidden mysteries lurks in the oceans deep.
Some will be discovered; others' secrets are for the earth to keep.

The sea batters the beaches
as the tide flows in and out,
and the waxed moon smiles and caresses
the sand with moonbeams of light.

A Single Flower

Soft-petalled roses revel in wonder
as the light from the heaven's cascade throughout their souls,
and the daffodils join in their ballet.
As the nectar of nature injects its essence of life and smiles as they
emerge whole.
Oh, to be a flower, absorbed within its own perfume
only to die momentarily and be reborn again and again.
Oh, to be a flower, swaying with the gentle summer breeze
and dancing with the rain.
A gift of a flower is to give beauty, a gesture of appreciation and caring.
The scent of a flower is to have it absorbed into one's memory,
to remain everlasting and sharing.
Let us pray for the continuance of nature's abundance of glory and
wonder,
and let us pray that the earth will prevail and that no destructive force
will put
asunder.

The Rose

I lay quietly upon my bed and gazed thoughtfully at the ceiling.
To my delight, I saw the flower unfold before my eyes.
The richness and redness of the rose was striking.
I experienced a new surge of passion race through my body,
and I smiled in anticipation of the dance of each petal,
as it harmonized with the gentle breeze that passed by.

A gentleness exuded from the firm, regal center of its soul,
and I saw the tiny trickle of wetness slowly travel along its delicate
frame and
dance along its stem, and I licked my lips with its perfumed taste.
My eyes teared as I felt its sudden pain,
and each petal grew limp in the paleness of death,
Draining its very essence, and I cried for its short life and for the waste.

Mist

She moves gracefully through the forest christened by the sunlight filtering
between the trees, a flowing whiteness of mist hovering above the water,
moving within the flowers.
Scents of perfume are left behind as she permeates
within the green walls of the hills.
Every trace of her is there, buds open with the joys of her touch.
Leaves even surrender, and fall gently to the ground, willingly giving
themselves to the soil.
Bumblebees fill their cups of nectar until ecstasy is achieved in their
hives,
and the birds chant with joy until they can sing no more.
Her bare feet are caressed by the wet moss leaving it dry, as trees
sway, rivers rush by, insects prepare themselves to die.
A mystical shower of glory and wonder emerges, each and every day
in our world, it is life, it is nature, and all that this planet unfolds.
If you look, smell, and taste all that it is, it will enchant you
as it is yours to behold.

Nature's Prism

The sweetness of life invaded my senses,
and I inhaled deep within its perfume.
The touch of such exhilaration
inspired my wildest thoughts,
and I thanked God for this gift of life,
and the planet for its cocoon.

I saw the flowers, a delicate and colorful array,
landscaped against the sunset, joyfully dancing in the breeze.
The warmth of the sun caressed the sparkling waters of the lake,
and laughter was echoed through the trees.

The birds of the sky soared high,
sending messages of thanks for the earth that God had built.
I saw the wondrous shades of each color imaginable
stretching far as the eye could see, like a giant patchwork quilt.

The Cure

It's a fragrance that exudes from the warmth of the leaves.
It's a crispness that gives lightness of step
and opens up your soul to receive.
I feel the droplets of truth pour from my eyes;
in a sudden gush of emotion, I understand.

Nature is a cure for all ills,
a caress for a much-needed touch.
It's a softening essence, a soothing lotion in motion.
It permeates your skin on a hot day from the sun,
and through it all, our father is on watch.

Erosion of Faith

As the barren lands grow hard and cracked,
deprived of the precious touch of rain,
faith in life appears to diminish,
and with it vanishes the only dreams that remain.
Plush green folds belong only to the pictures of yesterday
and are replaced by the stark reality of today.
But who can we blame for this pain inflicted on the human species?
How did we bring ourselves so much despair?
Ignorance and total exploitation of nature itself,
so much damage and so very difficult to repair.
We have to awake to the knowledge that we are in alignment with all
species,
animals alike, from the second of creation we have all been the same.
When will people awake and begin thinking of all humankind,
and the Earth they inhabit? We must cease to continue to play the
stupid game.
If we do not, life as we know it will cease to exist,
and too soon we will be soaked into the earth from whence we came.

Mystical

Searching for My Father

Where has the glow gone? Did it flee yesterday?
How did it wane? Was it slow and unseen,
or was it quickly whisked away?
As a tree torn from its roots,
I was not sure where I belonged.

Can I find my inner connectedness once more?
Dare I risk the answer? Maybe he doesn't know me, maybe I'm wrong.
As the sun shines and gives warmth, the colored petals reach out,
and the life essence secretes within the rose's stem
down into the earth, and then blown into the wind to rise into the sun.

My purpose of living and the growing process
of finding my reflection of life has graciously just begun.
I need to feel I am one with one,
even when physically alone and only I.
I need to kiss the life of my extension
to set me on my journey as a union until I die.

Touch of Love

The peace flowed through the membranes of my mind,
and I overflowed with the joy of love
as a certain essence mingled with mine.
I felt new and elated as I swayed with the frequency of time.
I gazed over the mist of truth and saw the blueness of the sky,
and his touch was a softness felt.
Never before had such sadness filled my nerve endings,
and yet the buildup of love ached deep inside of me.
It was only then that I knew of the true life that surged within me,
and how I could reach out to touch the divinity of myself.
The chanting I could hear was unrecognizable, almost mystical.

Final Resting Place

Two hundred years had to pass, and my journey would at last end,
and my destiny written for me by the guardians of my soul
would emerge raw and real.
Confused by my mission, so many discoveries oozing through my memory,
constantly puzzling me with the sensations I had begun to feel.
It was written I was to come, and the greatness would be in my mind,
of whom truth would only know.
The teachings have shown me how unearthed passions and mystic illusions
have allowed me to grow and expand my mind.
I was anxious about what visions would I finally see
as I soared though the galaxies to this earth, which was to be my resting place.
Would I be able to emerge victorious to lead souls, without pain?
Led by me, would they see the truth, or with closed eyes turn truth to lies
written on my face?
It was said that only blackened souls would be left with white brittle bones,
zigzagged over the barren land.
But a miracle would exist, a small group of wise men would be there, survivors
allowed only by God's hand.

Works of Nature

Mystical tears fall like raindrops from the sky,
and as through the eyes of a child
I am spellbound yet know not why as
I enter into a world of wonderment
never known before, and as I approach,
it's with a friendly fear.

As the visions appear before me,
the golden birds soar upward through the air.
I look with so much anticipation
and feel God at that moment, held there.

Cosmic Pull

Mosaics of marble pillars standing tall and strong
As I walk through the walls of warmth.
A knowing inside that I do belong.
Flowing robes, with posies in my hair,
sandals on my feet, and a gift of the veil for only me to wear.
I stand at the foot of the bed
and reach out to touch his hand.
It has just all begun, the cosmic pull to that unforbidden land.

Withdrawal of I

I smell the lust and travel higher and higher,
and I taste the blood in my mouth, and hear the cry from my lips.
The exulting carrier of ecstasy devours my flesh,
folding gently my senses into one small droplet,
and travels along to my fingertips.
The silkiness of your body holds me firm with anticipation,
and I feel the flow of your liquids mingling with mine.
It's so astounding to my mind as the hands enclose my soul
and squeeze harder and tight.
I'm breathless as the wetness pours down from my calves,
and droplets of nectars descend down over my body,
bathed in a pale pulsating light.
My breath ceases, and my body slides away from you
as the force urges me on, beckoning me to stay,
but the loneliness is terrifying as I lose what I am,
and the acceleration takes you further away.
I cannot accept that loss of my own essence,
for I am not yet ready for time travel,
for I cannot grasp back what it so greedily taken.
Did I let go too soon, or should I have stayed longer?
For maybe deep inside of me, I am too afraid to look.

Disbelief

It was as if I no longer existed, and yet I felt a touch and caress of
another soul.
And yet as beautiful and exciting as it was, I denied its captivity as I
chose to
be aloof so as to stay with you, where I remained whole.
To what great power touched me, and traveled throughout me,
seeding an essence so pure, yet with no face, I do not know.
Yet now the drainage of my own milk has left me weak,
and a sacred part of me has vanished without a trace.
I descend thankfully back into completeness of my body.
I am indeed different, for within my egg of secretion of desire, there is
a void, an empty space.
I feel the aftermath, yet the aftermath of what, I truly do not yet know.
Yet I acknowledge an absorption of power as it tugs me to and fro,
urging me to let go.
I could still feel your body on mine, the droplets of wetness running
wild
into each crevice of my being, wildly turning me inside out.
Your silkiness appeared as if a coverlet of fur,
as each fine hair and its dance was reflected inside of my eyes,
and the sweat of your body trickled into my flesh.
My lungs dissolved, no longer providing me with air,
and I prepared myself to die.
But my eyes opened; it had been a lie.

The Revelation

The peace that passed over his face was full of beauty and allure,
I felt my resignation and realized it was a welcoming journey through the cosmic door.
He was light-skinned and had features that would have not been said as kind,
yet in death, hidden in that face, there was a smoothing line that, if you looked for it, you would find.

The knowledge that life is gone in a wink of an eye
makes me live today with a smile on my lips and my heart soaring so high in the sky.
If you can love yourself and find that love within,
then for you there is no death, only the knowledge He is living for you, and life is now.

Beauty, Sadness, and Wonder

We must always pursue and search for the truth, step into the unknown,
and revel in discovery.

Dancing flames of sheer delight and vivaciousness of colors fill the
starlit skies, kaleidoscopes for eyes to see,
and droplets of warmth find their way hastily back to earth,
bringing tears to my eyes.
The death of a comet a necessary wonder of the cosmic story,
a chance for all humanity to observe and share a mystery.
A wonder to exalt in its wonderful glory,
thousands of stars twinkling in the moonlight night.
Clouds travel effortlessly through nature's beams of mystical light,
and owls hoot their messages to other night creatures flying high in
the sky.
The ecstasy of a firefly is witnessed with great sadness as you watch its
fragile existence fade and die.
So many wonders and mysteries have been placed in front of our eyes
and faces.
So many hidden riches and awesome sights lurk
in unexplored and, as some people think, forbidden places.

The Return

The bleakness of the night has disappeared
through the walls of my mind,
and as the dawn broke through, I cherished
the return of the joy inside myself.
Forces of passion for life are returning tenfold as I open my eyes.
The glow is deeply encased, bringing warmth to my soul.
And I am grateful for your presence and willing ears that hear my misery.
I am now myself totally and completely held in your hands, together again, whole.

Invisible

The mood is mellow,
and the night stretches into eternity;
for me, the passage of time is no more.

I am suspended in time
as I gaze listlessly into the mystical emptiness
of the air that surrounds me.

I feel as a ship stranded on the shore;
all is around me, yet I walk unseen
through visions of beauty and light.

And as impatient as I become, they see me not
as I walk totally alone and powerless to fight.

Abandonment

Born Again

Growing old and left alone;
eye sockets filled with cold and despair;
no glimmers of warmth, no food, no human love is there.

The chill invades the house,
seeping into the dampened cracks in the walls
and filling the air with winter rain.
It seems sadder this year, each time false hope,
only to have the loneliness repeat itself again and again.
They say the memory is a wonderful thing.
Aye, so it is, yet somehow it gets stuck in the chills of the past.

When you feel the joints stiffen as in my old bones,
it seems more difficult to make the good memories last.
I feel kind of strange now, and yet
there's a stillness and a sudden want that I finally feel.
The aches have gone, long forgotten.
I'm awoken to finally become real.

Punishment

To shatter a dream that was carefully held
in a hand of love and warmth;
To bring chills to the fiery embers of the heart
is to rape the body and mind of hope, of a future envisioned,
sometimes in the most beautiful fantasies.
To reject a heart offered unselfishly
is to batter and bruise tendrils of true love and desire,
is to not deserve the need, wants,
and endless love that a human touch can unfold,
placed delicately in the soul.

The Teachings of Life

The voices of truth
carry their words to each and every corner of the world,
a race against time for them, but they are relentless
in their pursuit to ensure that the truth be heard.

Messages sent in all languages
for each and every mortal who walked the earth to hear.
A reaching out with love and peace, a holy kiss for each.
The touch of a hand to have a friend when you feel that awesome fear.

So much chaos, confusion of right and wrong,
many overwhelming themselves in sin.
The missionaries were there to listen and to guide,
to show the people where to begin.

I say unto each and every frame
where inside exists the sturdiness of truth and honesty.
To trust your ability and the ability to share your strength,
to teach that infinite wisdom,
and give life by teaching the art of truth.

Primitive

It's another long and dusty road,
another end with no reason; it's just another day.
The air thickened by my guilty act of seemingly treason.

I desperately hang on to where I feel should be the place I belong,
but as I grip tighter, my hold appears to weaken instead of becoming
strong.
I am lost in the mist of chaos and foreboding chills.
I do not feel the sun warming the plateau, only the surrounding
darkness of the hills.

Inside of me lies a primitive being,
the cry of a raw and inflamed flesh against skin.
The beginning of time will not elude me,
for I no longer hold the key from how we begin.

Numbness Returns

I tried so hard to let my head rule, but my heart took over.
Are you so blind? Can't you see it's part of a cover?
Tears fall heavy now, are they pouring down my face?
There will be no winner in this race.
Why do I need you, and why can't I be loved?
Why did you always say goodbye?

Constriction of my heart tells me the truth; we are better apart.
I hear the laughter of days gone by,
but I still feel the joy on my face of a summer rain.
The odor of lust invades my senses,
and you are there, giving yourself too.

The remnants of lust and need are gone,
numbness returns, yet I am filled with gratitude
that you are forever gone.

Reminiscing

Remembering You

Rising passions flood the fertile landscapes of my mind.
All my fears and disillusionment of yesterday's love have been left far
behind.
I am now complete in the bonding of life for a man and women to share.

And as I revel in the joy of discovery of love,
I receive such pleasure to bare to you, my love,
and hope you understand how much I do care.

I always knew what love should have been to feel,
and maybe now that knowledge has been enhanced since the day we
first
touched, I only knew of immense joy and pleasure.

I can honestly say that all of the moments we have shared
have been absorbed and held gently in my mind and heart,
will be forever remaining there for me to treasure.

It is possible that you can be caring, sincere, and true,
and that there is someone who truly desires your touch and gestures,
who really does love you! Who?

Spiritual

I Am Going

I am going to breathe in your glory
and keep looking for you.
I am going to tell the story
that only your words are true.
I am going to keep looking
until you are here.
You have asked me twice to watch for you;
only your voice will remain sincere
when I see your footprint on the sidewalk,
in a circle of light.
Your face I have not yet seen,
yet I will know you by sight.
I will reach out to hold you in an embrace
as our hearts and minds once again will be filled with the beauty of
your grace.

Wanting

I feel so weak in that inner place
that has not yet been touched by life and air.
Carefully closeted and tightly held,
desperately trying not too share.

A priceless gem inside of myself,
wrapped in a cloth of glittered stars,
never seen in the darkness of the night.

The core of those jewels sparkle
with sensations and colors exuding wondrous prisms of light.
The walls feel suddenly thin, and I see and feel that aura of life
secrete through, holding love's touch.

And I boldly yet nervously pass over the box
to the guardian of my soul, and love,
begging that he understands
just what and whom he holds in His hands.

Seeking a Thread

Within every soul, there is a need to reach out and be understood,
to be weak and know that way is all right.
With every dream as it diminishes, leaving the fear, there just has to be
somebody there to hold you in the darkness of the night.
The beauty of being as one when you give your body
and mind, knowing that you are truly together,
is also to be aware that you are needed without a single word being
spoken,
and you will be held safe forever.

Is it right to expect or assume love will automatically manifest that
expressed
emotion, or am I bad and wrong to desire a truthfulness of devotion?
Should I be disillusioned and choose to plant the seed of doubt in my
mind?
If my force of love, and a spiritual union is by another unreturned,
should I feel rejected or humiliated, should my soul withdraw,
lost and spurned?
To be aware of another's needs is a journey inside of yourself and
an adventure in feeling and giving,
but if your selfish desires are only for yourself, and you are oblivious to
the needs around you,
then sadly you are alone, for it is not life that you are living.

Responsibility

Let us pour the cups of truth through the lips of our children,
and let them experience the texture and taste.
Let us teach the true meaning of life
and show them the futility of war and its terrible waste.

Instead of mistrusting one another,
let us reach out and clasp their hands.
And let us sing from our hearts and, with the spirit of God's love and caring,
Ensure His voice is heard in all lands.

The Star

It looked down on me, hypnotizing me with blue-green shimmer.
Yet each time I looked, it appeared different,
sometimes more intense, sometimes more of a glimmer.
Somehow the star that shone up there appeared to be much more than
it was;
it appeared to talk to me with gentle words.

The message was impounded on my brain
yet with a softness that is difficult to describe,
and with each murmur and foreign sound I heard,
I knew it was a shining star of hope.

No man could put up with murder, or destruction of good;
it's there for all humankind to look up into the heavens
and fill that spark of ethereal warmth and glow,
the way a human eye should.

It's a sign of an ethereal presence as every prism of light is shed
upon the earth's fertile soul.

Loss

Seeds of destruction are implanted in my breast
as my heart cries out in the birth of the morning sun.
I am lost in a fog of terror, it crawls through my flesh,
and even my nerves chatter; the only thing left to do is to be motionless, as the
rain turns blue.
Then I breathe deeply; normality returns again.

Whirlwinds created by nature's unrelentless need for normality
continue on forever and a day.
Her dream to once again arouse the earth
with the gentle touch of dew, to be engulfed in the glory of a moving mist,
and touched with the ray of sunshine, bringing warmth and life
that even through time will never fade away.

Fading of Life

I first saw him through the waterfall in my eyes, motionless,
bent over with overwhelming despair.
The clock in the hallway pulsating more with life
than the forlorn creature sitting there.
My tears scorched my face as I felt his inner helplessness,
and a clamminess invaded my heart.
I sensed more than I saw: that only a tiny flicker of life burned
within him,
but his soul would soon depart.
I burned with anger, wanting to understand
how this mortal frame had become so alone.
Was his sin growing old and wrinkling with age?
Did we only care for the young and those unmarked by life's experiences,
or did we forget simply to turn life's page?
Why was it so difficult to care for dying eyes and ears that could not
hear?
How selfish people had become, and how blind we were to give in to
another—
such darkened chaos, which would never become clear.
I pray for all humanity, young and old, that we stop neglecting our own
images.
We must allow our hearts to reach out to all with love, to show we care.
Let us promise that we will always be ready to open our arms, ready
to hold
and ready to share.

We Are

We are delicately made, with a trimming of lace,
big brown eyes, never lost in the beautiful face.
Tear ducts as a petal of a flower caressed by tiny droplets,
continually falling hour by hour.
Gazing ahead, that angelic form, so petite and small, innocent of all.
Why must we grow up and find the world is not as we want?
The most precious of love remains untouched even by truth.
A maze of pictures that we build in our minds is not really what we see,
or what we know we shall find.
We give ourselves to those we think take our offering gladly
and with sincerity will return unto us.
When it is too late, we find that the form became twisted,
and the mirrors were no longer there, but our lesson was learned.
After the tears, we are to see the truth stripped bare.
The secret of sharing our mind and soul
Is always to do it with another's timing, having enough time to remain
whole.
Take the good and ignore the bad, remember the times it made you
laugh,
forget when it made you sad.
It is their loss, whoever they might be, to have decided to turn their
backs.
No one can have their white knight in armor; those fantasies are what
they are.
But to be able to just love is a rarity, and we must assume it's returned.
To make the perfect cream or cheese that tastes as nectar,
so should we be churned.

Looking

I woke this morning, my face wet with tears.
Past pain has been cleansed, and now things are clear.
I prayed to the sky for a good man to appear in my life,
but sometimes it's not clear because you dare not take a step,
because you are full of fear.
I asked for someone like you to come into my life.
But the sky's messages in reply is not always what you think.

I want to tell you that I want to
Laugh with you, kiss your lips, yes!
I am ready to even take a chance.
This will begin only when the ethereal in me will ask you to dance.

Wanton

Although the passion arises so deep and a tidal wave crashes through my flesh,
I need you to perform your dominance in every lustful way.
I know that your lips do not caress mine enough.
I need the secretion of your mouth so as to be absorbed into mine, forever to stay.
I want you to take longer, exalt my being with a slowness,
and for me to absorb every flutter of your heart.
And I want to look deep into your eyes and talk as your feelings probe,
reminding me that as of today, we will never be apart.

I know I demand an awful lot, but my desires continue to arise as the oceans
and crash upon the cliffs of my soul.
I have so much to say, and I bubble over with a secretion of fermented liquid,
with the cream of life, and mixed with you, I emerge total and whole.

My nostrils twitch as I absorb the perfume of your body
and feel the stickiness of you trickle against my hand.
The throbbing of the life within you moves against me,
and I hear a sound escape your lips as we journey to a plain in a forgotten land.
Your tongue moves effortlessly into my mouth, and I hold back my desire,
careful, for I do not desire to hurt you.
Each movement perfectly lined, building to a crescendo of passion.

My Cosmic Fortress

Louder than a sonic boom and more powerful than the pull of gravity itself,
experienced by only a chosen few.
A flame spreading with such precision into the walls of my cosmic fortress,
each ripple mounting with the force of a tidal wave.
For you and I encased within the bubbles of life,
floating on a clear liquid of love, pulled, wrapped, and imprisoned willingly
and joyfully into a mountain within a cave.

I left my love, my being, and traveled beyond
and deeper into my soul of cosmic knowledge than I have ever dared to go.
For now, I have encased the experience of your lust and appetite for my flesh,
and welcomed your touch.
I recognized the power not only of you but myself, and the next lesson should be more joyful.
Due to my trust in the divinity of myself and knowing even that level of ecstasy will be just too much.

Concerns

I think about your yesterdays and worry about our tomorrow.
Will it begin a gentle journey, or will the storm and chaos follow?
I know not of what you think; I cannot see the version you see.
And that's what makes me so afraid—are we to be or not to be?

I do not want you across my door,
I do not want your feet on my floor.
I cannot be kind with you
simply because you turned to crush such sweetness,
and dents you did leave.
And for that I give you nothing but bitterness.
I hold gently the child in my hand,
and for her, I tread not on your soul.

But heed this, and remember it well:
that we will be three together always,
without you, for we only are pure and whole.

Gazing across the Water

An encounter with the sea, its hypnotic song,
tempting you to ride upon its waves.

It pulls you down with its tendrils, as in ancient times
it devoured mighty men and slaves.

An enticing wonder of nature, yet as gentle as a baby,
yet as deadly as the death of a star.

Mighty mountains viewed from a planet beyond,
conceived with the thoughts of life, admired, but only admired from
afar.

A Visitor from Hell

The air was still, and no one stirred,
at least no one that you could see.
But in that room, there were demons at work,
feverishly working with one plan in mind:
to ensure I would never be free.
I had fought my way back from the dead
with relentlessness, cunning, and trickery,
each action bringing me nearer and nearer.
Yet even as my beloved lay sleeping peacefully
in the four-poster bed, unaware of me and my plight,
the animosity of my mission became clearer and clearer.
There, the purple mist surrounding them in the windowpane,
I eyed Torian, the demon of the sea,
one arm with the flesh dragging upon his hunch-like frame.
And sitting upon the bedpost was Lithian,
a demon much deadlier than most,
for it was from the inner pits of hell from whence he came.
I felt the pressure in the air and knew this, at last, was the moment in
time
that I had traveled this far, and I braced myself
against all that is black of the soul.
As I gazed straight ahead, I fixed my mind's eye
on the faint glimmer of light across the room, and the pull began.
I weathered the onslaught, and as I crossed the threshold,
bathed in incandescent light, I emerged a woman, made whole.

Unstoppable

Eight years, and thirty-six strong Welshmen said no to the deluge,
but to no avail; Parliament would have its way.
There would be no refuge.
The serene village of Capel Celyn would die as it was soaked to its skin.
The living and the dead would be removed,
nature's wonders torn from limb to limb.
A whole village, its school, the chapel, and cemetery where the dead
had lain to rest, each engrained in the land,
Was to perish under the onslaught of a cruel and rebellious wet hand.

The Choice

The fortification of hurt that seeps within when given the option to remove your dead,

knowing resistance is now futile, the law passed, and the agony is to begin.

The gravestones that for centuries kissed by the warmth of the sun and cooled in the chill of night

all bore witness to weddings and the shedding of tears as the now empty vessels sent their souls into the light.

But their resting place would be torn away, either by willing hands or an unwanted force, to churn into disarray.

The liquid essence for life would bring deep sorrows, drown away guardians of the past, storm the bones of the dead, a cruel and unrelenting hand.

For centuries the Welsh had lived, laughed, cried, and celebrated their language and their culture always, cherishing and nourishing their land.

The Wiping Away of Capel Celyn

Eyes' view of monuments, dark rich soil nourished by farmers, food kissed by nature's lips.

Stories of love at first sight, lovers running hand in hand across the undulating hills and at harvest time laughing in a field of hay.

The cries of a newborn baby in the neighbors' house, built in 1893. All these memories will be forever visually taken away,

remaining forever in the minds of the Welsh people; maybe a few photographs will be found, a sorrowing wistfulness of a raw day.

Removal men come to each house one by one, a job that has to be done, but all walk silently, stooping under the weight with eyes unusually bright.

As the last belongings are removed, doors are locked for the last time; anger seethes within. The kitchen windows will never again see the sun; they will forever be out of sight.

And then the day arrives. With scorching pain, they watch the water rise up and up. Grandfathers and grandmothers cling and mourn together.

Children full of fear, too young to understand, hold their fathers' hands. Babes cry in the arms of their mothers.

And now all is out of sight, nothing but wetness fills their eyes. Uncontrollably it falls as the existence of where they lived is wiped away.

The Gestures

Gravestones have been lifted up, vessels left to soak, only eight removed and given a new resting place of hope.

The chapel has been rebuilt with the skin of its beginning, yet the land has forever changed; hurt gives the power to maim.

We are born to suffer and born to die, and as humans we rarely see eye to eye.

It's hard to understand why this event had to be; it's hard to keep faith in God sometimes that I can understand and see.

But history speaks for itself: the Welsh are resilient, their voices are undeniably strong and, music to our ears, live life.

Know that when the stories of truth keep your memories alive, of your language and culture,

it brings a never-ending warmth of knowing who you are that it can never be put asunder.

The Decision

I had been sitting with my mother for over an hour, filling a vase with water for her tulips that I bring to her every Sunday.

This day was different. The weight that I carried in my heart was hard to bear and even harder to share.

"What would you want me to do?" I asked her with a tremor in my voice that hadn't been there before.

As I stared out over the water, I sensed her smiling at me, yet I knew her eyes could not see.

Her mind had been lost to me for ten years now, and my father was buried in the cemetery.

Soon this spectacular view would be no more, and I had been given an option to either remove or leave the dead where they were.

"What would you have me do?" I asked her again. I turned to face her and heard words from her voice.

"It would be so nice to visit your da, my love, and we could have a picnic; the cemetery is not that far."

It's unfathomable where that voice came from, but suddenly the burden lifted, and I took my dad to a new resting place.

And then on one Sunday my mother came along, and for the first time, she recognized my face.

Always Remember

Men and women huddle together at the edge of the water, against the coldness of day, eyes moist with remembrance.

A mist appears to hover over the reservoir's calm surface, as if trying to hide, but the bouquets of daffodils cut through its skin. It's for the ghosts who pass through its water, and for the people who lost everything, kin to kin.

The yellow cuts into its surface, creating ripples across the water, reminding all of what still lies in its depths.

Memories of passed ones remain in its deep, dark path as it journeys on its way to quench the thirst of others. I see the pictures of the old schoolhouse and the teacher, and maybe pictures can be found of the old chapel and its preacher.

Over fifty years have passed, but we must never forget water is a life-sustaining thread.

It is not a weapon to deprive a livelihood, sow pain, or imprison the dead.

CPSIA information can be obtained
at www.ICGtesting.com
Printed in the USA
LVHW040846250721
693543LV00001BA/50

9 781663 219671